TOP TALENT

How to Hire Your Dream Intern

NICOLE SERENA

Nicole Serena

Top Talent—How to Hire Your Dream Intern

Hire your Dream Intern!

If you want to hire the best intern, you need to know how to pick them from the pile of resumes sitting on your desk and how to coach them to their full potential. To do this, you need to follow a simple, seven-step process. This book is for managers looking to find and hire the top talent for their team.

In this book, you will learn:
- How to craft a job posting to attract top talent
- Where to find top candidates and how to identify them early
- Interview techniques to identify the intern that fits best for you
- Coaching tips and techniques for top performance
- And much, much more!

"The One Minute Manager" meets "Good to Great!"

Top Talent—How to Hire Your Dream Intern

To all my Dream Interns—past, present and future.

You are the inspiration for this book.

Table of Contents

Chapter One
My Story — How I Hired Dream Interns and Became a Superstar at Work

I am writing this book about interns from my own personal experience hiring and working with young graduates. I have seen the good, the bad and the ugly. Overall, it has been a great opportunity to expand my leadership and coaching skills, as well as succeed in my own department. I have seen young employees develop, grow and figure out the start of their career path. I have learned how much I enjoy working and coaching new graduates and employees, and what I can learn from them. They always have fresh ideas, know the newest technology and trends, and have a different outlook on the world. It is with these opportunities that come fantastic growth and enlightenment within organizations. Rather than looking at the next generation as a lot of work, I look at them as an opportunity for my department to grow and learn. So how did I get here?

Let me share my story

A few years ago, in my new role as Director within a Healthcare Company, I had a new department with a lot of projects to do, but NO staff. At the time, there was no opportunity to hire anyone in the foreseeable future. What was I to do? I could hire consultants who cost a lot of money to assist me with my workload, but I didn't have the budget to do much of that. In the past, in a previous job, I remembered that we had a summer student and he had been a great help. My nephew was also in his last couple of years of university and was going through his own internships. He shared with me the challenges of finding a good internship and why it was so important to his future. He gave me an idea! I thought maybe this could assist me with my dilemma. I was worried, though, as I thought my projects may be too "senior" for the students. I would be hiring someone who could do more than file some papers and do administrative tasks; I needed someone who could come into my new department and work on real projects. I had to think carefully about what the projects were, and what skills and competencies these students would need to be successful.

I wrote out the projects I needed and thought carefully about what I wanted them to do and what I would need to do myself. I also thought about the traits and competencies I needed my employees to demonstrate to be successful. I needed a self-starter who could work independently and without a lot of oversight. I thought to myself, "am I asking too much of a new graduate or student?" I remembered how I was when I was first starting out, and I would have loved to have the opportunity for these types of projects. I realized that if I went forward with this, I would need to place considerable trust in these young people.

A lot of people said that I was crazy to consider this possibility, because from their experience, summer students were a ton of work. They asked me why would I want to hire students as I would have to hold their hands all the time; I didn't have time for any additional work managing these students. I also didn't have much experience working with young employees, but how bad could it be? And I needed the help. Again, the word "trust" came into my mind and I knew I needed to try it.

I worked with our HR department and developed a job posting. The posting was very important, as I wanted to hire a specific student for a specific project. I didn't want just any intern; I needed my Dream Intern.

I waited and waited, thinking that no one had applied for the job. Then I was astounded to hear that 600 people had applied for it! WHAT?!! Luckily, I had support in HR to go through the pile and hand select ten for me to look at.

While this was going on, two applicants, who had done some research and learned I was the hiring manager, sent me an introductory email. Smart move! I was impressed with their tenacity to find me, and I added them to my list of interviewees. If they hadn't sent me that email, they probably wouldn't have made it to the top of the pile.

I had planned to hire one student and, in the end, I hired three! Two of them were the ones that sent me an email.

How I figured it out

From outlining the projects I needed help with to picking the right students, the interns went to work right away. And with weekly guidance, they were getting everything done and more! Yes, I was lucky with who I chose, but part of that was my process beforehand: taking the time to figure out what I needed, the capabilities I required, and the level of education necessary (I now usually hire Masters students).

I continue to do the up-front work before hiring students: planning what I need them to do, taking the time to develop the right job posting so it is clear what their responsibilities will be, and taking small amount of time each week (usually just 30 min/week) to keep them on track and on task.

The biggest reward I have had was to hire one of these students into a full-time job in my department. He is probably my hardest worker. I also enjoy assisting my students in finding their next job once their contract is complete. It doesn't have to be within my department or even within the company. My goal is to help these young graduates gain skills, experience and competencies to go out and be a huge success.

Working and coaching them throughout their contract is key. Sometimes they are not the right fit for my department, but working with them on their goals and strengths helps me and them determine where they want to go, and then I try to coach them towards that direction and future success. I have had students go on to become sales reps, analysts, physicians, recruiters and more.

Managing expectations is probably my biggest role at the beginning, throughout the contract and at the end—when they are leaving for another role or if I can hire them. I find everyone is much more open to challenges if their expectations are discussed from the start.

Why I want to help you

I am not only passionate about assisting the future workforce generation and helping them gain and develop experience and skills; I want to assist you with your talent challenges within your current workplace. I get excited about the potential for you to succeed and find your Dream Intern. This is something that I want to aid as many people with as I can.

I have developed a plan to identify, hire and coach interns, and I want to share this plan with you because I can only hire one to two interns a year and I want to have a greater impact. I want to see hundreds and thousands of young graduates have an opportunity to use their skills and gain the experience they require to find the job or start their career in a different way. Millennials/Gen Z—they are not that different than others; they are just growing up in a different working environment than older generations. It is harder to find a job these days for new graduates. They are more open to a flexible working environment, they think on their feet and they are used to contract jobs. This can make for a great opportunity if you are open to being flexible, too.

I hope that small, medium and large companies see the opportunities that interns can bring to their organizations: bright young talent that is willing to work and finish all the projects that are left sitting on your desk, inbox and mind. It is so exciting and a big relief when you can handover one of these projects to someone who is happy to take on the work. It is not their burden; it is their opportunity. What a win-win solution! As I have said before, it is my mission to encourage everyone to look for opportunities to hire young graduates and give them a chance to do great work.

Chapter Two

Introduction – Why You Need to Find a Dream Intern

Does this sound familiar?

No matter where you work, small business or large corporation, there is always more work to be done. Urgent, important, deal making, deal breaking—it piles up and you feel you are barely catching up. Only the fires are dealt with, while you look longingly at all the strategic work and opportunities that are just waiting for you. You can't make time or clone yourself, so how do you get it all done? With resources scarce, how do you succeed when you are drowning in the pile of urgent tasks that need to be completed? What is the answer to these issues? It's simple: find and hire your Dream Intern!

My guess is you can relate to the following situation. Maybe it describes you.

I have so much work piling up: if only I had someone who could do the urgent projects so I can get on to the important work. I don't have time to hire an intern as I am too busy already, and to be honest, I don't know how to do it. I wish there was a solution to my problem, as I know it would be helpful to have an intern, but I just don't know where to get started.

I need to find the best interns/summer students to support my business. The problem is, I heard interns can be a lot of work. The process is going take time. I don't know how to write a job posting, and then what do I do with it? What if I get stuck with a pile of resumes? I don't have time to interview and pick someone. I don't have time for this! And what if I pick the wrong person? That will make my life even more challenging.

Does that sound familiar? What is it costing you without your Dream Intern? Time, money, and success! It is also costing you the opportunity to coach and develop some amazing young talent. Identifying and coaching the new talent pipeline for your organization will not only assist you within your department, but also will make you look good to your boss. I have always been amazed how when my interns do well, I do well. Your status at work increases as you are seen as a leader within the group. Young employees, who do great work, reflect well on you. Even young employees who struggle can make you look good, as when you manage someone from struggle to success, not only do they feel great, you feel a sense of achievement as well.

Imagine having time to work on the projects that mean the most to you and your boss, and yet at the same time have all the other tasks and urgent work done quickly and efficiently. It seems too good to be true, but there is a way!

This book will be your guide on how to not only find your Dream Intern, but also how to manage them to great success. It will reduce the time and energy it takes as well as increase your success rate in finding great talent. Through worksheets, tips and techniques, I will guide you through a process that will help you identify your Dream Intern. It can also help you build your talent pool for the organization or small business that you work on.

Hiring your Dream Intern can decrease your workload so you can focus on the important work. It can make you look like a hero to your boss by completing the projects that need to get done that no one else wants to do. It can turn you from Zero to Hero!

Quick summary of what is to come

This book will be your guide on the process of finding and hiring your Dream Intern. We will work together to structure the project, develop the job posting, select the top resumes and manage the interview process. We will then work together on a process to select your top candidate and to offer your Dream Intern a great opportunity they can't refuse. Once you have hired them, we will work on how to manage them to get their top performance and you will be celebrating the work that they finish. You will have hired your Dream Intern! Let's get started!

Chapter Three

The Solution – Quick Overview

I am so excited you decided to buy this book and discover the steps to success to find and hire your Dream Intern. My goal with this program is to show you an easy and straightforward method that will not only encourage you to hire a new graduate, but also make you look awesome doing it!

Let's discuss how we are going to find and hire your Dream Intern.

There are seven key steps to follow, and we will work together throughout this book.

Here is how you do it: a quick and easy summary of each step.

1. Setting Up the Project — In this chapter we will work together to identify the work that needs to get done and develop potential projects that your intern will work on. This is the most important step of the whole process. Identifying what work you need completed will assist us in identifying who your Dream Intern is. It is also important to figure out what expectations you and your company have of your new intern and outline these within the project.

2. The Job Posting — We will develop an exciting job posting that Dream Interns will be interested in and identify key colleges, universities and other job sites that will want to post your opportunity. The posting will be based on the outcomes of step one and will build from all your previous work.

3. Reviewing the Candidates — Together we will review how to go through the candidate pile and identify your top candidates to interview. You will learn tips and techniques to quickly go through all the resumes and how to find help to assist with this process.

4. The Offer — We will discuss how to craft an offer your intern will jump at and that your company or small business can afford and say yes to.

5. Day One — Let's set up your Dream Intern's first day for success. Day one is your opportunity to start on the right foot. We will work together to plan the necessary steps to on-boarding your new intern and ensuring they start with all the tools and support they need to be successful. Managing expectations starting on day one ensures that there is clear and consistent communication throughout the work term. This is a key to success.

6. Ongoing Coaching — In this chapter, we will continue to discuss opportunities for success for both yourself and your intern. We will discuss how often to meet with your intern, what progress checks and development goals should be created, and how to manage issues that may come up and lead your intern to grow and develop. As mentioned earlier, managing expectations throughout your Dream Intern's contract will ensure they stay on task and that their project is a success.

7. End of the Contract — Finally, we will discuss what happens at the end of your Dream Intern's contract. What options are there afterwards for both of you and how do you manage the outcome? Working together, we will identify before you even hire your intern how you will manage the end of their contract.   If you know up front what you can potentially offer or not offer your intern is again key to their—and ultimately your—success with this project.

Once you have completed all the steps within this program and book, you will be on the road to finding and hiring your Dream Intern.

I am so excited to start working with you!

Please note that I have developed this book to go through all the steps for success in hiring your Dream Intern on your own. However, if you feel as you are completing the exercises or going through the book that you need additional coaching or assistance, please reach out to me at <u>nserena.scc@gmail.com</u>.   I would be happy to continue to work with you to ensure your success.   I have additional coaching and workshop opportunities to assist you in a more one to one or small group environment.

Chapter Four

The Project

"Today is full of possible"

Understanding what you want your Dream Intern to do within their contract and clearly identifying their project is the most important step in the process. You want to outline and know who your Dream Intern is and what they will be working on. It is important to take the time and energy to do this right. Plan to spend at least two to three hours on this step to ensure success.

Within this chapter, we will go through three steps; outlining what you want your intern to do, the competencies and skills that are required, and finally what your vision of success is at the end of the contract.

Going through each of these steps will help you define and identify who you want to hire and what you want them to do. I have seen people hire interns because they can, but do not prepare for them and ultimately do not get top results and are disappointed. This is not the intern's fault. How can they be successful if you do not illustrate what you expect of them from the start?

Defining the project

Let's start by looking at *worksheet A*, "defining the project." To begin, think carefully about what you would like to get done that isn't getting done right now. Don't worry if you think it is too difficult for an intern; this might be your contribution. The idea is to outline everything and then figure out what you can get done once you have the time—after you have hired your intern. Take about 15-30 minutes and write everything down. Don't criticize your thoughts; write it all down. You should have at least ten to fifteen items on your list. More is even better!

Second, using *worksheet B*, categorize the items into each of the following: critical, important, nice to do and wish you could do. Then organize by type of work: admin, strategic or operational.

Note beside each item how often these need to be done. Categorize by the following: daily, weekly, monthly, and quarterly.

Finally, identify which of these you can assign to an intern and which you need to do. Carefully consider what you can delegate. This is key to the exercise. Be prepared to delegate tasks and projects that you at first would not consider. You can oversee these and teach someone else so you can get to the most important work.

When you have finished the worksheets, you should have a rough idea of what your intern project will look like. This will be the basis for your job posting, as well.

If you need to gain upper management approval for your intern, use *worksheet C* below and develop the framework for your project proposal.

You are ready for the next step!

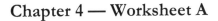

Chapter 4 — Worksheet A

List all the tasks and projects you need to get done:

List all the projects that you wish you could get done but don't have enough time or resources to do:

Chapter 4 — Worksheet B

Look at each item on the previous worksheet and categorize below. Then add how often each needs to be done: Daily, Weekly, Monthly or Quarterly.

Administration:

Strategic:

Operational:

Chapter 4 — Worksheet C — The Intern Proposal

Goal: In 1-2 sentences, describe the goal that will be achieved by hiring your Dream Intern.

Outline: Briefly outline the tasks and projects from *worksheet A* and B that you have identified in one to two paragraphs.   This will assist you in selling the opportunity for your company to hire your Dream Intern.

Budget: What is the salary for your intern?   Also include benefits, equipment and any training costs.

Return: If possible, can you quantify the outcome—saved time, money, efficiency measures, etc.

Chapter Five

The Dream Intern Posting

"Your Dream Job Posting does not exist; you need to create it"

In this chapter, we will discuss how to create the ultimate job posting for your Dream Intern. We will discuss what to include in the posting, where to post it and develop a timeline for the posting. Let's get started!

Developing the ultimate job posting

First off: there are many articles, books and experts who will tell you exactly how to structure your job posting and the words to use. What we are discussing here is the pre-work before you write the posting. I have said it before: the preparation and thought before developing the posting is the most important part. You need to be clear on who you want to hire. Have a clear picture in your head of who they are and what they are going to do for you before you write a posting.

Review the worksheets you have already completed and remember what tasks and projects you need completed. Think carefully about the level of intern you are considering; do they need a Masters or PhD? What are the characteristics or competencies that are crucial for success within the job and your organization?

Start to develop your posting, whether you have a stock posting that your company develops or your own creation after you have completed the worksheet at the end of this chapter. It will give you a good outline that you can drop right into a template you already have or it could be the basis for your posting.

You need three sections within your posting: a description of the job, the requirements for the job, and the timing and contact information needed to apply.

Part one — the job description

Using the worksheet at the end of the chapter, outline what exactly you want your intern to do. Be as concise as you can, but at the same time detailed enough that your potential candidates can decide if they are qualified for the job. Outline some of the key values, job expectations, and the type of attitude that is valued by yourself and your organization.

Requirements to apply

List the minimal requirements for the job, including education and any specific digital or computer program requirements that are crucial for success. I suggest you be precise in what you need. If you want someone able to do pivot tables in Excel, include this in the posting. You do not want to get surprised on day one when they only have minimal experience and you need an expert.

If you want someone with very specific skills, outline in the posting that there may be a test or that you want proof of these skills. This will help ensure they have the requirements and do not waste your time.

Timeline and contact info

Outline at the end of the posting the deadline to apply and be specific that late applications will not be accepted. Be firm on this;

if they want the job, they will meet the deadline. Also add in a contact email or drop file box where you want the resumes sent. I suggest you do not use your personal or work email. Set up a separate email account if needed and then the applications will all be in one spot together and not lost within the mountain of regular emails you receive. It will also be easier if someone is assisting you with the process, as they can have access to this email box rather than forwarding every application on. Finally, it is better not to give out your email address as you do not want to be inundated with emails trying to get additional information about your posting.

One final note: I suggest you add to the job posting that only the top candidates will be contacted for an interview and thank everyone in advance for applying.

Part two — posting the opportunity

To find the best candidates, you need to post your opportunity in the right places. It is important to think carefully whom you want and where they might be. Is there a particular college or university that you would like to hire someone from? Most schools have recruitment officers and would be happy to speak with you about their current candidates. Check in with your HR department as your organization may be affiliated with some graduate programs.

Look at job posting sites and LinkedIn, as well. If you decide to post on any of these, be prepared for a lot of interest and a lot of resumes that may not match your ideal intern. You need to be very specific on large posting sites with high traffic on what you are looking for and who your ideal intern is.

Another opportunity for finding your Dream Intern is through word of mouth. Send the posting to your friends and colleagues and let them know what you are looking for. Ask them if they know of anyone finishing school and looking for an opportunity. Make sure they know what type of requirements you need so they send you the best potential interns. Discuss the opportunity as often as you can, as getting a referral from someone you know can often yield the best candidates.

Part three — developing the timeline

You are almost ready to finish your Dream Intern Posting. The final step is to make a timeline from job posting to hire date. It can take longer than you expect to find and hire your Dream Intern. It is important to consider this and start early on the whole process. If you want them to start in June, then begin the process three to six months in advance. Yes, I mean start this process in January. The best interns are looking for their dream job or internship as soon as possible. If you wait until near the end of the school term, your top candidates may already have an internship and will be busy with their final exams. This is a stressful time for new graduates and knowing they have their dream internship beforehand leads to greater success for everyone.

Now that you have completed all the requirements, post that job and get ready to meet your Dream Intern!

Chapter 5 — Worksheet A — Job Posting Outline

Description of the job — outline exactly what the job is and what types of activities the potential candidate will do throughout the internship. 150-200 words are ideal.

Requirements — outline exactly what education and skills are needed to do a good job and if there are specific characteristics or competencies you want—please be precise. Finally, if there are higher level skills/experience that are preferred, list them as well, specifying that preference will be given to those with these qualifications.

Education:

Skills:

Programs:

Characteristics/Competencies:

Chapter 5 — Worksheet A — Page 2

Timeline and contact info:

How long will the posting be up?   (one to two weeks is usual):

List contact info — (email is best):

Posting —make a list of all the possible posting opportunities: include university and colleges, job posting sites, bulletin boards, company posting services, recruiters, friends and colleagues.

Chapter 5 — Worksheet B — Job Posting Timeline

Develop a timeline from job posting to hire date:

Date of posting:

End of posting:

Set up interviews:

Conduct interviews:

Decision and job offer:

Start date:

Chapter Six

The Candidate — The Resume Pile and Booking the Interviews

"Talent will get you in the room, character will keep you in the room"

— Unknown

This is the exciting part after posting your job opportunity: seeing all the resumes arrive into your inbox (or your HR inbox). Allow for at least two weeks as you compile them. What you are looking for are approximately ten good candidates to review in more detail. The best interns usually have applied to multiply postings and you want to be prepared.

If you don't get a good response to your posting, consider waiting another week or look and see if there is somewhere else you can post it. It is important to get this minimum number of ten candidates to find the right one.

How to handle the pile of resumes

First off, congratulations! Your future intern is probably within this pile of resumes! Let's get started reviewing how to go through them.

Did anyone reach out to you beyond applying? If yes, then put them on the interview pile. A candidate that can find the hiring manager and send them a personal note is a person who goes above and beyond.

If you have the resources, have someone else go through the pile, reviewing each letter and resume based on the job posting. Ask them to pick out the top 20 resumes, and then you can review these in detail. If you have a good response, you can always go back if you don't like the first set of resumes.

Are there any that do not have a cover letter? They should go to the bottom of the list. I prefer to read the cover letter and if it is well written and looks to be aligned with the posting, I put them on the interview list.

Do they meet the minimum qualifications? If not, again, put them on the bottom of the list.

Have any of them done a project or job similar to what you are looking for? Top of the pile.

Keep going until you have your top ten candidates. You need ten as some may no longer be available and after your first round of interviews, you may need to interview a couple more.

Contact your top four first and book the interview. They should be eager and available when you want them. Be flexible, but if someone is very specific and makes it tough to find a time that meets their schedule instead of yours, move on to the next candidate. You want someone who wants to work for you and is eager to meet you. Being difficult booking an interview maybe foretelling of how they would work with you in the future.

The interview – interviewing for success

There are many books and articles on how to do a job interview. You may even have certain guidelines to follow depending on the company you may work for. This is not what we are going to talk about here. You have probably also done interviews before and have some favourite questions you like to ask.

My question to you is: besides developing a set of questions to ask a candidate, how else do you prepare? If you haven't in the past, don't worry; this is what we are going to prepare for in this chapter.

First off, review the worksheets we have completed so far. Remember what projects and tasks you want to be done and what you are looking for in your intern. Consider what type of questions you would like to ask based on this review.

Let's go to the worksheet at the end of this chapter and begin the exercise.

List the key tasks and/or projects.

What two questions would you ask based on this? Write these down. I suggest one of the questions would ask the candidate about a past experience and how they handled a previous project. If you don't get enough information, ask another question to clarify.

Secondly, list off the key traits and characteristics that you believe are important for your new employee (i.e. resourcefulness, integrity, reliable, etc).

Write down two-three questions about this; again, ask for examples of previous experiences that show these characteristics.

Finally, write down two-three questions what your interviewee may ask you.

Think what you would ask if you were in their shoes. After each question, write down how you would answer these.

Tips and techniques

If a candidate struggles with a question, give them encouragement and time to answer.

Ask the candidate how they found the job posting and why they are interested in your company.

Consider having a second person in the interview with you. They can take notes and ask key questions. It will also give you additional insight into a candidate.

Keep the interview 30-45 minutes long and schedule fifteen minutes after to make notes while the interview is fresh in your head.

If you can, have someone else meet the interviewee and bring them to the interview room and then accompany them out. This will give you time to prepare before and after. It will also keep you on time if you have multiple candidates.

Finally, if you know within ten-fifteen minutes that a candidate is not a good fit, end the interview early. Do not waste your time trying to fill the entire interview time slot.

It's time to meet your dream candidates!

Chapter 6 — Worksheet A – Interview for Success

List your top ten candidates by preference:
1.
2.
3.
4.
5.
6.
7.
8.
9.
10.

First 4 interviews—include date and time:

1.
2.
3.
4.

Chapter 6 — Worksheet B — Key Interview Questions — What Do You Want?

Project/task oriented questions:

Key traits and characteristics:

Questions to ask:

Questions you may be asked:

How would you answer these?:

Nicole Serena

Chapter Seven
The Job Offer

"Happiness is a job offer letter!"

The intern offer

Great job! You have gone through the pile of resumes to find your top ten candidates and then completed the interviews of your select group to narrow this down to your top three. Whether it took one or two rounds of interviews, you are finally ready to send your Dream Intern their job offer. This is an exciting time and it is important to not only have a great written offer, but also a great process to inform your future Dream Intern. You want to get this right so they are excited and immediately say YES to your offer.

As I have said before, most companies have a standard template for job letters. We are not here to recreate what you already have; we are going to prepare what you want to put in the offer. It is not only how much they will get paid, but also the other factors that can be just as important to your future employee.

Look at salary ranges for new graduates with the level of education and experience you are hiring. You want to give a fair offer. Also, be prepared to have a slightly higher offer, because based on their past work experience or current living environment, an intern may ask for a higher salary. Depending on the city, state, province or even country, there may be minimums to pay interns and you also want to ensure they earn enough to live comfortably. You do not want your new top intern distracted by their home environment so they can give you their top performance. Look at what you would pay an entry-level employee; this can be your starting point. Decide on what the time-period of the contract will be. If this is a summer term then it is usually three-six months in length, or if your intern is a new graduate consider a twelve-eighteen month term.

You may also want to consider whether you want to add the opportunity for a renewal period of an additional three-six months within the contract. This may be a considering factor in getting your top choice of candidates.

Consider vacation pay, health insurance and other benefits, and flexibility in working hours as all being part of the compensation package. This may be one of their first job offer letters and they may have lots of questions. Be available or have an HR colleague available to answer any questions. Also, clearly spell out how and when they should return their offer and include any additional information or documentation that is required for employment.

You also want to have your top three candidates chosen. The first one may not agree to the offer or might have already accepted a competing offer. Be prepared to work with any of your top three.

The call

These days most companies send offers through secure email; however, I still think it is important to call your top candidate and congratulate them with the offer. This personal touch can go a long way in the work environment you are building with your Dream Intern. It should be a short call of approximate three-five minutes, congratulating them and giving specifics on how the offer will be sent.

> **Tip: You do not have to give a lot of details on the phone. Instead, suggest they read the offer letter and set up a follow up call to answer any questions and to manage their expectations.**

Be clear in when you need to receive the written offer back in order to secure their place. Remind them that all the information is available within their formal offer.

Managing expectations

Often your future intern will have a list of questions. I always recommend they review the contract and information your company provides first and then to set up a second call. Ask them to send you any questions beforehand so you can come prepared to answer them. Even if they accept the offer, it is still wise to have this call before day one. It will give you an idea if they have any areas of concern or uncertainty before they start. If you are unable to answer a question, send them to someone else (HR or personnel department), or get back to them after with the answer.

Tip: It is always better to respond later if you are unsure of an answer.

This call will continue to build your new working relationship with your Dream Intern and start on the path to success!

Chapter 7 — Worksheet

List the salary and benefits within your offer:

How many hours and weeks is the offer?:

Do you want to put in a condition for renewal at the end?:

What questions do you think they may have after the call? Write them down and consider how you would answer them:

Nicole Serena

Chapter Eight
Dream Intern's First Day

"The expert in anything was once a beginner"

— *Helen Hayes*

Good news! Your Dream Intern has accepted your job offer and will be starting in a couple of weeks. For them to be successful, it is good to prepare beforehand for their arrival.

Let's review some ways to ensure they start off on the right foot.

Before day one (at least two weeks)

No matter if you are part of a small, large or one man show, it is important to start as soon as possible so that their workspace and equipment are ready on day one of their new job.

Is there any paperwork that is required for tax purposes beforehand? Many states and provinces have programs that support businesses that hire young employees. These may give grants or tax breaks to support hiring new graduates. I encourage you to look in to these and see if you qualify.

Where will your intern work within the organization? Do you have a workstation set aside for them? What equipment (phone, computer/tablet, other tools and supplies) is required for them? It is much easier if this is all organized before day one, as the worst thing is hiring someone and then they are not able to get work done for a couple of weeks because their laptop/tablet (insert any other important equipment) was not ready. This has happened to me and can cause a delay in your project and potentially de-motivate your new intern.

If you work for a big corporation, you may have an on-boarding process that you need to follow, as well. Ensure you are familiar with any corporate procedures or policies when hiring a new intern.

Also ask yourself what training they may need to complete during their first week on the job. Is there any corporate or safety requirements that need to be done? Preparing for all of this will ensure an efficient and successful start.

On the worksheet at the back of the chapter, make a list of what needs to get done with deadlines and who is responsible. As items are completed, cross them off the list.

First day orientation

We all remember our first day on the job—butterflies in our stomach, excitement and apprehension that we will do a good job.

Your first actions of the day will guide and support your new Dream Intern. Make sure you are there to welcome them on arrival, or have someone to do it for you. Take them on an orientation tour of the office environment they will be working in. Show them where they will be sitting and the location of their new colleagues and team. Let them know where they can take their lunch and breaks, as well as any local options for lunch. Also ensure they know where the washroom and other amenities are located.

Return to their desk area and review any computer programs and other equipment they will be using with them. Give them around 30-60 minutes alone to get acquainted with their workspace and environment before their first formal meeting.

Set up a meeting with your team on the first day: this could be mid-morning or over lunch. If you do not have a team, have a one to one meeting to get started. Also arrange introductory meetings with other colleagues throughout your organization during their first week. This will give them a good idea of who is who and what different roles they play within the company. It will also give them an idea of who to go to with questions and support as they move forward in their project(s).

Managing expectations

Within the first couple days, set up a longer meeting (one-two hours) to review the project(s) your intern will be working on and answer any questions or concerns they may have. Prepare a list of questions you think they may ask and any you may have for them.

> **Tip: Continue to have meetings frequently for the first few weeks. Your intern will appreciate your support at the beginning, and as they get established you can meet less frequently.**

It is normal that your intern may start to ask more questions about the company, as well as their current and future role, as time goes by. I find it helps to ask more questions to learn more about what their goals and plans may be. Help your intern understand how their work impacts the organization and why it is important. They may question their small project compared to what other senior colleagues are involved in and get side tracked on wanting to work on additional projects.

Taking the time before and during the first few days of your Dream Intern's start can have an impact to the success of their project. Congratulations for taking the time to prepare!

Chapter 8 — Worksheet — Day One Preparation

List all tasks or paperwork that should be required before your Dream Intern starts: (add due dates and timelines, crossing off as you complete them).

Paperwork/forms:

Equipment and set-up requirements:

Meetings with colleagues/team members:

Required training and deadlines:

Initial 1:1 meetings:

List any potential questions your new intern may ask:

Nicole Serena

Chapter Nine
Ongoing Coaching

"Tell me and I forget, teach me and I remember, involve me and I learn"

— *Benjamin Franklin*

There are many coaching books and courses out there and all have their gems of wisdom. The biggest lesson I have learned from working with my Dream Interns is learning to decide when to coach and when it is time to manage. Coaching happens most of the time, but there do come times when you need to step in and manage your intern. The most important thing that I have learned and can share with you is to be supportive. Listen more and ask many questions. It is easy to tell our young employees what to do; however, they learn best when they figure it out themselves.

To assist with this chapter, let's review a few terms first:

Coaching: supporting an intern to achieve a specific personal or professional goal by providing training and guidance.

Mentoring: a relationship in which a more experienced or more knowledgeable person (Manager) helps to guide a less experienced or less knowledgeable person (Intern).

Managing: refers to the job of overseeing the work of an employee/intern to achieve goals and objectives for the company.

Now that we have reviewed some key terms, let's get started on coaching your Dream Intern.

Setting up a meeting schedule with your intern

I find that setting up a schedule with your interns gives them a sense of structure and guidance. It also allows them to know that is their uninterrupted time with you. Most managers and directors are too busy to hold hands with their intern. I look for a self-starter who just needs guidance through scheduled meetings weekly or biweekly. If you leave them alone longer than that, they could get off track, discouraged or distracted. I usually book 30 minutes, and no longer than one hour if needed.

Once you have had your initial meetings and set up their objectives for their work term, discuss and mutually agree on how often you meet. Agree that this time will be uninterrupted and you are there to coach and guide. This is their time to ask questions, get advice and learn from you, their mentor. Yes, you are their coach and mentor.

> **Tip: have your admin book these meetings in your calendars for the full time, and keep it at a set day and time. This will become a routine and build trust and loyalty.**

Performance reviews

I always find my interns are more successful when they know what their outcomes are for their work term. Set clear and concise objectives that are mutually agreed upon. I recommend three to five key objectives: any more than this and they will have too many to handle. Have your intern write them up and have ownership of how they are tracking to meet these objectives. Plan to meet every one to two months to go through these in detail. Document progress and areas for improvement. Allow enough time so that your intern can ask questions and show you their work. These meetings are longer than your one to ones, and should take 60-90 minutes.

> **Tip: Book your Dream Intern to do a formal presentation to senior executive as part of their internship. This not only gives them a chance to practice presenting but also showcases your Dream Intern for future opportunities. (And when they do a great job, you look great too!)**

These written reviews can be used in the future by your intern to show the work they did, the progress they made and their success, which they can discuss with future managers and employers.

Managing issues

As with any employee, issues may come up with your interns. I find it best to deal with them as soon as you notice it, and not let it simmer over a longer term hoping it will sort itself out.

Most issues tend to stem from misunderstandings or miscommunication. Have a quick meeting to discuss what is going on and to figure out a solution. Ask questions and try not to offer a solution too quickly. Guide your intern to find their own solutions; this will help them grow more independent and figure out how to manage it next time.

If there is an issue that cannot be coached, you must then consider how to manage the issue. Is it something that HR can assist with or do you need to take corrective action? I have found if I go back to the original objectives that were agree upon at the beginning of the term and get recommitment, most of the time things work out. Always consider there may be something going on outside of work that may be impacting their performance.

Career planning

As part of being a coach and mentor to your Dream Intern, the topic of career planning should be discussed throughout the internship. During the performance reviews and one to one meetings, openly discuss your Dream Intern's career goals and aspirations. Ask them to plan out what they would like to do in the next year and five years. Coach them on what is possible and how to work to achieve their goals. If they are interested in a sales career, suggest they ask a sales person to take them out for a sales call to see what the job is really like. Training opportunities and mini projects that can assist them in growing and learning about different aspects of their current environment will assist them in learning what they like and don't like doing. Early on in their internship they should be planning their next step, whether it is within your company or outside. Encourage them to prepare for after the internship ends. A success for you is when your Dream Intern moves on to their next dream assignment.

Chapter 9 — Worksheet — Coaching

Setting up the schedule:

Book your 1:1 meetings — how often will you meet?:

Performance review:

Outline the main three-five objectives for your intern:
1.
2.
3.
4.
5.

List out their career aspirations and goals—how can you help them achieve the next step?:

Chapter Ten
End of the Contract

"With every end comes a new beginning"
— Anonymous

All good things come to an end at some point and so will the time with your Dream Intern. Whether it is six, twelve or eighteen months, when their contract end draws near there are decisions to be made.

Some companies plan to hire their interns after a specified period and others will finish the contract and then hire a new intern. The important thing is to be supportive and give your Dream Intern a lot of lead-time to make decisions for the next step of their career.

Begin speaking with them at least two months before their term is over. If you are interested in extending the contact or offering them a job, let them know as soon as you can. The best interns are making plans from day one of their internship and if you want to keep them, make sure you know. Encourage them to look at the internal job postings, as well. If there is a position they are interested in, encourage them to reach out to the hiring manager and meet with them before they apply. If you are planning to extend, try to give them a one-year contract. This will assist them with gaining experience and will also be easier for you for planning.

If you are not planning to extend their contract, give them advanced warning, too. I have found this is the time they need the most support as they need to start planning the next stage of their new career. Give them feedback and encouragement on their strengths and areas for improvement. Even if you are not keeping them, continue to encourage them to plan and look for another job. Ask them what they are interested in doing and help guide them. Suggest they meet with other people to ask about their careers to get insights and suggestions. Sometimes these introductions lead them to their next opportunity.

Plan time about one to two weeks before the end of their term to go over their final performance review or appraisal. Suggest to them that they gain feedback from other colleagues and to bring this to your meeting together. It is also very beneficial to have your Dream Intern do their own self-appraisal of their project or work term. They should document and review their areas of strength and consider areas for their own personal improvement.

Ask them what they thought was their greatest achievement from their project and remind them to use these examples with future employers. What was their biggest learning opportunity from their time working with you? And finally, ask them what one to three things they would do different next time? This self-reflection is very important in growing through their career.

It is then time for you to give them further insights and suggestions from your observations over the past few months. Your comments should not come as a surprise to them, as you have been meeting on a regular basis with your Dream Intern. Be honest and give them clear examples so they can understand where they did well and how to improve. Suggest books, courses, podcasts and other resources that they can continue to learn and gain insights from.

This is also an opportunity to gain insights from them as well. Ask them what they enjoyed most from their experience and if they have any suggestions for future internships.

Finally, when it is the last day of your Dream Intern's term, make sure to celebrate them. Recognize their achievements with team, take them out to a final lunch meeting or have a small reception with the colleagues they worked closest with. If you can, give them something to remember their work term with you, whether it is a card that everyone signed or a small memento from the company or team.   Plan to have as positive of an ending as was their beginning.

Chapter 10 — Worksheet

What is your plan after the internship is complete?:

What were the successes and learnings from this internship?:

What would you do differently next time?:

Tip: **ask your Dream Intern if they would like a letter of reference to keep on file.**

Nicole Serena

Chapter Eleven
Conclusion

Congratulations! You've made it to the end of the book—and the process for finding and hiring your Dream Intern.

Let's do a quick summary of the steps to hire and coach your Dream Intern to success:

1. Set up the project.
2. Develop and post your Dream Intern job posting.
3. Review the stack of resumes and select your top ten candidates.
4. Invite up to four for interviews.
5. Offer your new Dream Intern a great job opportunity.
6. Day one starts for your new Dream Intern.
7. With continued coaching and support, your Dream Intern will do a fantastic job on their project and make you look like a rock star.
8. At the end of their term, you will continue to support your Dream Intern through the process to their next step, whether that is with your current company or something completely different.

May this book support and inspire you to continue to hire Dream Interns for years to come!

My hope for you is that with this program you will find an easy and straightforward method that will not only encourage you to hire a new graduate, but also make you look awesome in the process.

I believe I given you all the tools and worksheets required to get you started on your journey to find and hire your Dream Intern. Continue to use this book as your reference guide throughout the process and into the future.   You can get a free emailed copy of all the worksheets on my website at http://www.dreamintern.ca/.

If you feel you need additional support and coaching, I would be honoured to support you. Please email me at nserena.scc@gmail.com and we can start working together.

In conclusion, remember to celebrate the success of you and your Dream Intern and all the progress you have made together.

Further Reading

Great at Work – Morten Hansen
The Coach – Steven J. Sewell and Matt M. Starcevich
The Power of Moments – Chip Heath & Dan Heath
The Difference – Angela Lauria
Finding Time to Lead – Leslie Peters
H3 Leadership – Brad Lomenick
Tribe of Mentors – Timothy Ferris
School of Greatness – Lewis Howes
Radical Candor – Kim Scott
Not Taught – Jim Keenan
The 3rd Alternative – Stephen R Covey
How to be Here – Rob Bell

Acknowledgements—Thank You!

To my wonderful family, who supports me in all my adventures and experiments in life.

To my life partner, my husband Andy, who trusts me when I do not trust myself and encourages me to keep going when I question myself on what I am doing. Thank you.

To my children, Sara, Josh and Sylvia. I am inspired to encourage the world to embrace the future generation of interns who will bring energy, new ideas and excitement to each new project and opportunity.

To James and our conversations about interns, and the initial idea for this book and the next one!

To Becca for being my proof-reader and editor! I couldn't have finished without you!

To The Author Incubator, Angela, Cheyenne, Chela and all the supporting staff. Thank you for supporting me on this book-writing adventure and for pushing me to write and finish this book!

And, finally, to the Archangel Summit 2017. Thank you for inspiring me to write my first Moonshot, which is where this book idea came from. It is amazing to see how writing down an idea can bring it to fruition!

About the Author

Nicole has a passion to support the next generation of graduates and interns. She has spent the past 25 years in corporate life and

has hired her fair share of them. She has been a speaker at healthcare conferences in North America over the past three years.

She specializes in helping leaders, managers and entrepreneurs find and hire their Dream Interns. She knows first-hand how an intern can get the work done that has been on your "to do" list but never seems to be crossed off.

Nicole currently resides in Ontario, Canada with her family. She enjoys spending time with her family and finding time to practice yoga, meditation and taekwondo.

She is an avid reader and the creator of <u>Nic's Book Blog</u> on Instagram, which features her reading adventures. You can follow her @<u>nicsbookblog</u>.

Thank You

Thank you for taking the time to read Top Talent—How to Hire Your Dream Intern. If you have made it to this page, you are ready to hire your Dream Intern.

I would love to continue to support you on your journey. Please visit my website at http://www.dreamintern.ca/ to download a free checklist and a PDF of all the worksheets within the book to support you through your hiring process.

You can also contact me via email at nserena.scc@gmail.com for continued coaching and training opportunities.

Good luck with your next Dream Intern!

Notes

Made in the USA
Columbia, SC
20 September 2022

67494693R00048